Edwin Catford's EDINBURGH

by
Alan Brotchie

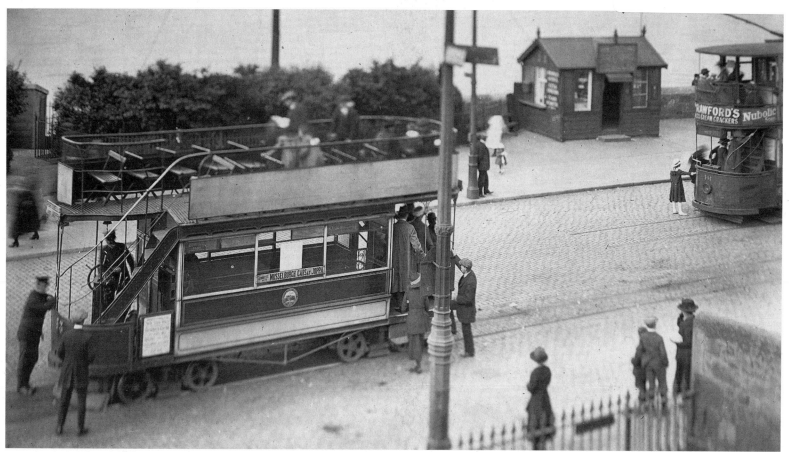

At Joppa the cable trams met the electric trams of the independent Musselburgh Electric Tramways which ran through the 'honest toun' to Port Seton. Waterloo Place to Joppa was the final cable route to be electrified, the last cable car running, unlamented, on 23 June 1923. The tracks were connected at Joppa, and Edinburgh cars began a joint service to Port Seton. This photograph, taken before work commenced to join the two lines, shows cable car 53 on the left (itself a rebuilt former horse tram), and on the right a very unkempt Musselburgh car, No. 16. In the background is the primitive waiting room.

First published in the United Kingdom, 2004,
by Stenlake Publishing Ltd.
Telephone: 01290 551122
Printed by Cordfall Ltd., Glasgow, G21 2QA

ISBN 1 84033 322 7

**The publishers regret that they cannot supply
copies of any pictures featured in this book.**

ACKNOWLEDGEMENTS

My sincere thanks are due to EOC's daughter-in-law, Mrs
Margaret Catford, and his grandson Ken for their help.

Unfortunately the glass negative of this charming study has been
broken, but it still shows fine details of the controls of one of
Edinburgh's cable tramcars. The shadowy figure inside the lower
saloon is probably the driver. Car 50 dated from 1908, and was
one of twelve built to a generally similar design in Edinburgh &
District Tramway Co.'s Shrubhill workshops. The vertical capstan
wheel was used to grip or release the continually moving
underground cable. Conductresses were introduced in June 1915
to overcome the manpower shortages occasioned by the First
World War. This picture was taken at Craiglockhart terminus.

INTRODUCTION

Edwin Osmond Catford (known familiarly as EOC) was a 'genial and inventive, modest and unassuming' man from a large Quaker family, who produced a remarkable photographic archive of transport scenes in Edinburgh in the 1920s and 30s. During this period he worked for the Transport Department's electrical department at Shrubhill works, but not as their official photographer. Nevertheless, his job gave him the insider knowledge to be where matters of interest were unfolding, and his photographic legacy provides a unique record of the formative years of the Corporation Transport Department. EOC passed several hundred of his half plate glass negatives to D. L. G. Hunter, who in turn gave them to me for safe keeping. They will be given a proper permanent home in the Scottish Life Archive of the Royal Museum of Scotland.

Much of EOC's work covers Edinburgh's tramways, and a brief history of their development is appropriate here. The city's first tramway opened in 1871 and was horse-drawn in those areas of the city where gradients permitted, with cable-hauled trams later operating on its northern hills. At the end of the nineteenth century Edinburgh's horse-drawn trams were also converted to cable operation, with the steel cable housed in an underground conduit between the tracks. Both horse and cable-operated tramways were privately operated, but by the end of the First World War the system was completely worn out and the owners had insufficient funds to undertake the necessary repairs. To provide an efficient transport system, the Corporation acquired the private undertaking in 1919 and proceeded to create an effective, state-of-the-art electric tramway which over the years contributed handsomely to the relief of the rates. EOC worked for both the Edinburgh & District Tramways Co. and Edinburgh Corporation.

Born at Saffron Walden in Essex in 1878, Edwin Catford was educated there at the Friends' School. He moved to Edinburgh in 1907 when he entered the service of the Edinburgh & District Tramways Company as their chief electrical engineer. It may be considered that holding such a post with a steam-powered cable-operated tramway was a sinecure, but EOC did not treat it as such. His testimonial from the general manager, C. W. Shepherd, on leaving the company's employ in July 1909, paid tribute to savings of over £160 per annum achieved in the electric lighting and power installations. EOC was involved in the preparatory work for the tramway company's Slateford electric route (its sole foray into electrification), but had left Edinburgh by the time this opened in June 1910. He had, however, demonstrated his inventive nature in several practical ways before that date by designing electrically operated signals

for single line tramway operation, which while never used by the cable tramways were later adopted to good effect on the electric tram routes. Another innovation was his 'Automatic Cable Fault Finder' which he patented and installed at Shrubhill power station. The moving cable (nearly four inches in circumference) which ran underground and to which the trams were attached for propulsion was, as it aged, liable to fray. When this happened all sorts of problems followed: the cable could get caught on any one of the numerous guide pulleys, or, on occasion, a tram would be unable to release itself from the perpetually moving force – with disastrous results! EOC's fault-finder employed prongs set $\frac{1}{32}$ inch outside the diameter of the cable, with broken strands setting off a warning bell. This allowed the engine driving the cable to be shut down and the problem to be resolved before chaos ensued. Unfortunately it was found that splices tended to increase the thickness of the cable by more than $\frac{1}{32}$ inch, thus triggering the bell, so what was a sound idea proved too refined for the standards then in place.

From July 1909 until March 1916 EOC was chief electrician and keeper to the States of Guernsey Lighthouses, a position to which he also brought his inventive flair, being personally responsible for the equipping of the offshore Platte Fougère lighthouse with a remote controlled foghorn. In this context he also investigated the unusual atmospheric distortion which can affect sound waves in foggy conditions. Edwin's first son (Edwin Frank, known as Frank, born in Guernsey) was a poorly child, and when told by doctors that he should be kept in the open air all day EOC invented what may have been the first baby alarm: beside the pram situated some twenty yards from the house an open telephone line was rigged up with a clock (to register that the line was 'live') making crying instantly detectable. The technique must have been effective as Frank Catford grew up to serve many years as depute town clerk of Edinburgh, while EOC's second son, John (Ian) became a university professor in Michigan. EOC's two cats also benefited from his ingenuity – a shelf by the front door was fitted with a switch triggering an electric bell, so to gain admittance all that was required was for them to jump on the shelf and ring the bell – a trick soon learned.

EOC's successes in Guernsey led him to contemplate emigration to the USA, but for some reason he did not qualify for citizenship. America's loss was the gain of future transport historians in the UK, however, and in 1916 he returned to Edinburgh. By 1920 he was employed as chief electrician of the Corporation Tramways, playing a major role in the electrification of the old cable lines. The new department, run by R. Stuart

Pilcher, had a major task to achieve, but one which was nonetheless accomplished with acclaim. EOC photographed many events associated with this transition, but unfortunately only a few negatives from the period have survived – there are even tales that some glass plates had their images removed so that they could be reused in greenhouses and cold frames!

Pilcher's paternalistic control of his department led him to encourage the establishment of many social and sporting clubs, from the mutual improvement society, savings association, pipe band, minstrel troupe and choir to golf and football clubs – each of the latter playing against their opposite numbers from Glasgow Corporation Tramways. The yearly golf match competed for the Maule Cup, presented by the then convener of the tramway committee, Robert Maule, proprietor of one of Edinburgh's first department stores, situated at the west end of Princes Street on the corner now occupied by Frasers.

One of Pilcher's ideas was for a staff magazine, the first number appearing in January 1923. Two years later editorship of this passed from Mr J. Telfer to EOC, who undertook this onerous additional (unpaid) task for almost twenty years. The quarterly magazine became *Speed (A Journal for all Lovers of Edinburgh)* from the beginning of 1926, then *New Speed* in 1935. It ceased to be published at the beginning of the Second World War, having reached a print run of 4,000 copies at its peak. The magazine contained many photographs taken by EOC, plus numerous articles of general interest, and achieved a considerable following outwith the transport department.

On his return to Edinburgh EOC was also appointed demonstrator in electrical engineering at Leith Technical College, fulfilling this post with distinction until 1935. He was additionally a fund of knowledge for the Edinburgh Transport Society which flourished before the Second World War. A paper by EOC about the effects of fog on sound waves won him the Keith Medal as the most important contribution to the Royal Scottish Society of Arts in 1937.

EOC retired in March 1938, but continued to edit *Speed*. He died in 1941, his funeral attended by a large turnout from the Transport Department. It is in his memory that this collection of his work is presented. Many more of his photographs are reproduced in the books by D. L. G. Hunter which detail the history of Edinburgh's transport. These would be much the poorer without EOC's legacy on glass.

EOC's first involvement with electric traction centred on the isolated electric tramway operated by Edinburgh & District Tramways Co. from June 1910 (although he had left the company in 1909 before the trams started running). Four former cable trams were converted to electric operation on the route from Ardmillan Terrace to Slateford. The cars chosen for conversion were apparently just those that happened to be in the works at the time, and as a result their numbering was random. Here No. 64 (the others were Nos. 28, 38 and 74) is at the Slateford end of the line, with the distinctive pagoda-shaped roofs of McEwan's Maltings in the right background.

Slateford electric car No. 28 'posing' in Princes Street at a time when this was entirely the province of cable trams. The purpose of this 1917 exercise was to demonstrate the appearance of electric cars if and when they were permitted to operate along the thoroughfare. The trolley pole is being discreetly held in the appropriate position by the trolley rope and the photograph was later augmented by the pole and overhead wires (this doctored view can be seen on page 11 of D. L. G. Hunter's *Edinburgh's Transport – The Corporation Years*). Edinburgh Castle looms through the mist, with the Royal Scots Greys monument at the foot of Frederick Street in the foreground. There are at least four versions of this view, each showing different spectators.

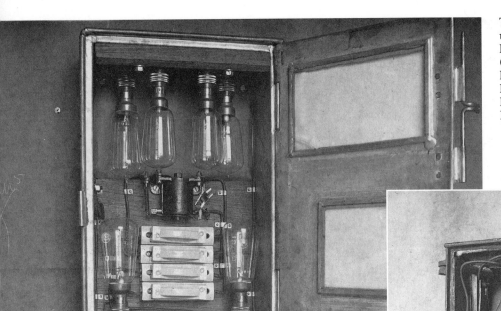

This picture shows EOC's design of single line signal lamp as used on Edinburgh's tramways. Illumination of the top (red) light indicated 'car approaching on single line', while the lower (blue) light indicated 'car going same direction as you on single line'. A provisional patent was applied for, but dropped. These lamps were in use at the Stanley Road and Trinity Bridge single line sections until the end of electric tram operation in Edinburgh.

EOC's signal superseded this model, which required a current of 5 amps to activate it, while two plungers see-sawed into solenoids activating a 10 amp switch. The improved design operated with just ½ amp and had a single moving part. Additionally, this old style model provided only a red 'stop' signal, which was less effective than the arrangement which allowed succeeding cars to travel in the same direction.

In September 1920 one of the first bus routes to be opened by the Corporation began operation from the cable tram terminus at Craiglockhart to the village of Colinton, passing the newly built Redford Cavalry Barracks on the way. This sylvan scene showing Colinton Road looking west at the barracks' gate is of interest not only for the early bus (Leyland SG 1650), but also the smart cavalryman, with sword drawn, at the gate. On both sides of the road behind the blurred couple are the level crossing gates of the temporary railway, which was built for transporting building supplies during the barracks' construction.

Edinburgh Corporation bought its first charabancs early in 1919 to meet a demand after the First World War for tours of the city, which either ran to the northern suburbs or to the south. Here Craigmillar Castle is being visited on the latter tour in the summer of 1920 using Leyland SG 53. The castle is probably one of Edinburgh's least visited historic monuments, and although now well within the city sprawl it still maintains a timeless atmosphere. Constructed from local sandstone, the well-positioned fortification was a defensive seat of the Preston family from the fifteenth century and saw visits from Mary, Queen of Scots. Inhabited until the mid-eighteenth century, the extensive ruins well deserve more visitors than they presently receive.

A national coal strike in 1921 created a potential crisis for the cable tram system, which depended entirely on four coal-fired power stations for its operation. Problems were initially avoided by large stockpiles of coal being bought for Shrubhill power station, and the collection of additional supplies of fuel direct from the pits. Tollcross power station was converted to use heavy oil, but eventually tram operations had to be curtailed. Things returned to normal in June. Having temporarily been converted to a lorry, one of the first Corporation Leyland charabancs (S 9258) is seen being hand-loaded at an Edinburgh Collieries Company pit, possibly Preston Links. This scene is unusual as the photographer's shadow appears in the image!

Thirty buses were ordered by the Corporation for use while the 'northern' cable car lines to Goldenacre and Comely Bank were reconstructed for electric operation, and some of these were fitted with a primitive run-back preventer to give confidence on the steep hills encountered. Four AECs are seen here in Henderson Row, parked opposite the former cable tram depot and power station. The depot was used for a while as a bus garage, but never again for trams. Although they remained in place for many years, the tram tracks in Henderson Row were never used by the electric trams. Other than Morrison Street, this was the only stretch not converted, as even in cable car days it was only used as a link to the depot.

This picture shows one of the early Leylands on the tram replacement service from Waverley to Comely Bank, photographed in East Fettes Avenue near the old tram terminus. SG 2140 (No. 35) was unusual in that its bodywork was built by Lincoln Lorries Ltd. of Louth. On reconstruction to electric operation, the tram terminus was extended some 400 yards west, to beyond Orchard Brae.

Although slightly older than the vehicle in the upper view, Leyland SG 1651 (No. 24) presents a much more modern appearance, arising from its conversion from solid to pneumatic tyres. In fact this was one of the very first buses to have pneumatics fitted – in 1923. Its bodywork was built by Leyland, with several noticeable differences from that by Lincoln Lorries Ltd.

In 1920 experiments were carried out with front- and centre-entrance buses, most examples being reconstructed from vehicles with their entrance in the then conventional rear nearside corner. This is Leyland No. 28 (SG 2134), altered thus for one-man operation so that the driver could also collect fares on lightly used routes. The side board reads 'Bernard Street & King's Road', a route which started as a Saturday and Sunday only service from June 1921. Traffic superintendent Robert McLeod is in the front seat of the bus, but there is no record of the identity of the infant glued to the window behind him, or its male charge!

After considerable debate, a design for the centre poles to be used along Princes Street was agreed, and arrangements in which EOC was intimately involved were drawn up for alteration of the relevant trams from cable to electric operation. As much work as possible was done in advance, but cable cars continued in operation until midnight on 21 October 1922. 300 workmen – hampered by hordes of spectators – then immediately set to work. The thirty (pre-painted) poles had been laid out along the street, the holes to receive them had already been dug, and by 9.30 the following morning the first electric cars were operating. On that Sunday morning the new pole (which would subsequently carry street lighting too) contrasts vividly with its predecessor.

Looking east along Princes Street after reconstruction work has been completed. The temporary track which had been laid on the north side of the street has been removed, and the track on the south side still has a central cable slot (but it had been electrically bonded by this stage). The old fashioned lamp standards seen in the left picture have been replaced by two lights on each central pole, bringing a state of order to the street which has not been seen since.

Edinburgh's first double deck (i.e. top covered) electric tram seen on Gorgie Road on Sunday 22 October 1922, immediately following the conversion of Princes Street to electric running. The implication in EOC's handwritten caption on the back of the print is that open top cars travelled the route earlier that busy day. On the left of tram 192 (itself a former cable car) Robert McLeod, then traffic superintendent and general manager from 1935 to 1948, is again to be seen. To the right is the tramway committee convener, Bailie Mancor.

Leith, an independent burgh until November 1920, had an electric tramway almost twenty years before Edinburgh, but EOC appears not to have ventured north of Pilrig prior to the amalgamation! This scene, showing the Bernard Street swing bridge with the now trendy Shore beyond, dates from 1922/3, as the tram (an Edinburgh one) is on service 14, the Churchhill and Granton Circle, an extension of the former Granton Circle route operated by Leith Corporation. A (fixed) low concrete arch has replaced the opening bridge, and shipping thus can no longer proceed further south up the tidal part of the Water of Leith. Large vessels such as that downstream of the bridge no longer moor here, as the berth is occupied by a floating restaurant.

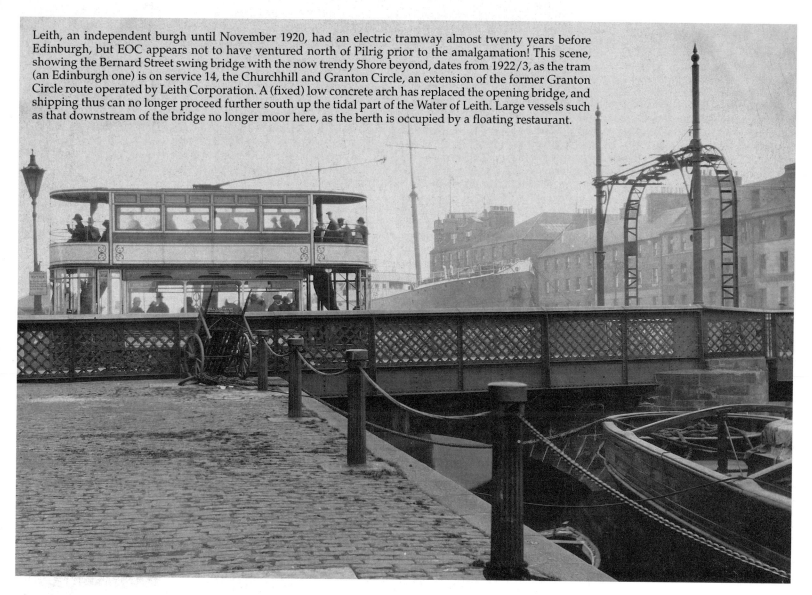

In June 1923 the Traffic Department held the first of its annual staff drives. The hardy souls travelled from Shrubhill to Perth in these three solid-tyred charabancs. The outward journey was via Stirling, Milnathort and Glenfarg; the return via Crieff and Dunblane (remember this was a pleasure outing!). A lunch stop was made in Perth where EOC took this photograph at the entrance to the station. His two sons travelled with the party, and can just be seen at the left-hand end of the second last seat of the furthest charabanc. His wife is in the same row.

With most of the hard work of conversion behind it, the Tramway Department embarked on extensions to the system beyond the old termini. One of the first of these to be undertaken was from Murrayfield to Corstorphine village, opening in June 1923, just three days before the last cable car ran to Joppa. The roadway was widened considerably (to the great benefit of today's traffic) for this new line. Here track-laying is underway near Balgreen Road involving a large labour force, plus an early mechanical aid, a 1-ton tipping 'Tructractor'.

The old northern routes to Goldenacre and Comely Bank were the last to be returned to tram operation following temporary operation by bus, to the severe annoyance of residents. The reconstructed Comely Bank route reopened on 18 November 1923, and this wintry scene was taken soon afterwards at the crossing of Queen Street and the foot of Frederick Street. A window board refers to the annual winter carnival held in the Waverley Market. The only other vehicle in sight is Stevenson Brothers' laundry van.

The last cable routes to be electrified – on 8 June 1924 – were from Goldenacre across Princes Street and up the Mound to Tollcross. These two formerly distinct routes were connected across Princes Street, and because of the steep gradients involved drivers were paid an extra ha'penny an hour. The Board of Trade insisted that cars on the two northern routes had additional mechanically operated track brakes, and that cast steel bollards were fitted to prevent any derailed car ending up in Princes Street Gardens. Here car 215 seems to have its saloon filled with young ladies on their way to James Gillespie's School.

The Corporation's trams were always well-maintained with the paintwork normally immaculate. Cleaning was undertaken every night and an automatic car washer was installed at Shrubhill depot. An early vacuum cleaner was also tried out. This picture shows the depot of the former Leith Corporation, near the foot of Leith Walk. The 'family resemblance' between the converted cable car on the left, and the newly built electric tram on the right, is striking.

EOC was instrumental in the design of the electrically operated three-way points controller at the General Post Office junction. Initially this was implemented for reasons of road safety, but it was soon found to bring considerable operational benefits at this busy locus. From the left the switches were for Princes Street, Leith Street and North Bridge. The Points Boy would have to keep his wits about him, with a constant stream of trams to be correctly routed. A small weatherproof cabin was later provided to give some protection in inclement conditions.

A similar but less complex points box was provided at the foot of Frederick Street, but as this was used only by trams on route 24 to Comely Bank the responsibility for operating it was much less onerous. This manned arrangement was soon abandoned and a pull-switch fitted to the overhead pole nearest to the junction, which the tram driver could reach from his platform. Note that the boy's uniform cap even has the correct 'Points Boy' title.

In the late 1920s Haymarket saw the introduction of a 'gyratory traffic control', indicated by the studs where the points policeman is positioned, intended as an early form of roundabout. What the contemporary road engineer would think of today's integrated traffic lights and multiple mini roundabouts can only be imagined. The hour is 11 a.m. according to the Heart of Midlothian FC memorial clock. Note the old cable tram tracks heading up Morrison Street below the saloon car on the left. These were only used for two weeks at the end of 1900 as the route from Lothian Road to Gorgie attracted minimal patronage. The line was never used for electric trams, although it would have formed a useful bypass for the congested West End area.

WEST END,
STOCKBRIDGE,
BROUGHTON R°
BONNINGTON R°
LEITH DOCKS

5

154

CORPORATION MOTORS

SF 6522

SG 6054

SS 2532

After experimental use of two London 'S' type double deck buses, the Corporation purchased four AECs with bodies by the Brush Electrical Engineering Co. of Loughborough, one of which is illustrated here. SF 6522 (fleet number 154) was photographed in Charlotte Square, even then in demand as a place for parking (although there were no ticket machines or 'blue meanies' in sight then!). At this time bus service 5 ran from Charlotte Square to Leith docks, but was soon extended at both ends. The vehicles had solid tyres when they arrived, but these were soon replaced by pneumatics, as seen.

During the General Strike of 1926, the heavy repair shop at Shrubhill works was turned into a dormitory for volunteer staff. While the efforts of the volunteers were welcomed, initially only minimal use was made of their services to avoid damage to vehicles and injury to persons. However, as the strike continued the number of trams was increased until by the end of the first week 150 were on the streets in safety. The tram on the right is one of the former Leith Corporation cars, rebuilt by the Corporation, while in front of it are stacked underframes for new trams yet to be built at Shrubhill.

Tram No. 3 (later renumbered 75), newly built in 1927, crosses the top of Craiglockhart Avenue as it heads for Colinton. Cars built after 1929 had the ends of the top decks enclosed, and earlier trams of the style shown here were all shortly modified to conform with these new standards. Craiglockhart Parish Church, built forty years earlier, was then still in open fields, so much so that Sunday school picnics were often held nearby, with participants arriving by tram. The extension of the tramway from 'Happy Valley' (Craiglockhart) to Colinton opened on 21 March 1926.

This blackbird's nest was found in the destination box of one of the last remaining open topped electric trams. Birds nesting in unusual places seem to have fascinated EOC, who also took photos of siskins making themselves at home in a model ship and a nest in the Shrubhill works hooter. A few of these open topped trams remained available as spares and were used for football match specials etc. To judge by the Gorgie destination, this one had last been in use to Tynecastle.

The work of the Parcels Department was well documented by EOC, including this shot of 'boy with barrow' (although more often parcels were delivered by small vans). With an expanding fleet of motorbuses the Corporation found itself in need of further accommodation, and in April 1926 purchased the Industrial Hall in Annandale Street, illustrated here. Described as an 'extraordinary folly', this had been built in 1922 as a replacement for the Waverley Market when the latter was considered unsuitable for industrial exhibitions. When the Corporation took it over, the entrances seen here were heightened to allow double deck buses to get in. It remains one of the nerve centres of Lothian Transport.

This photograph was taken inside the parcel sorting room at Annandale Street. One can imagine this bunch of characters getting up to some mischief given the opportunity! Rates for parcels were very reasonable, ranging from 3*d*. for up to 7 lbs within the city limits to 1*s*. 6*d*. for up to 56 lbs as far afield as Levenhall. Parcels soon shifted to the former gatehouse at the entrance to Shrubhill depot, while items for delivery could be handed to the conductor of any tram or bus.

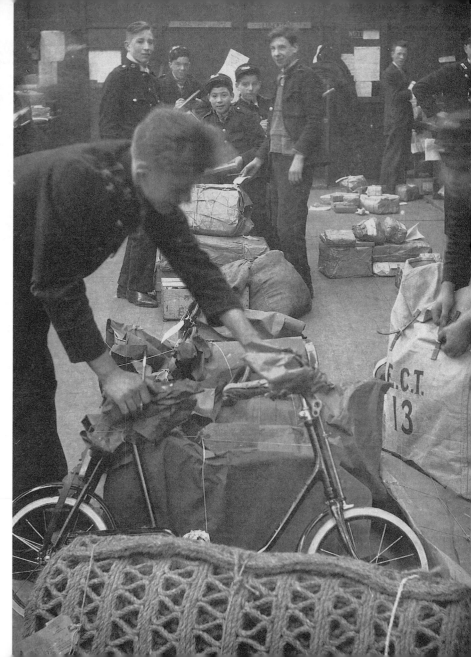

The interior of the former Industrial Hall following its conversion for use as the Central Garage. A fine selection of vintage vehicles is on display. The four Leyland Lions formed part of a batch of eight bought in 1926, while behind them are four open topped AEC double deckers, which, as can be seen, were then kept for route No. 5. In the far corner is a group of Leyland charabancs.

The electrical shop in Shrubhill works was EOC's domain. Having been converted within what had been the engine house driving the cables for the former cable trams, it was far from ideal. Here work on electric motors is ongoing, with facilities that could best be described as basic.

Staff dining facilities at the Shrubhill car body shop were also very basic. The reversible seats are from the lower deck of a tram, a table has been knocked up from old pieces of timber . . . and this was the provision for the collar and tie brigade, not the manual workers! On the left is Tom Mason, the foreman body builder who retired in 1930 after forty years service, having started his career during the horse tram era.

The Edinburgh tramways were remarkably free from serious accidents considering the city's hilly terrain. This one was more spectacular than serious, and occurred when the driver and conductor both left their car at Liberton terminus, the top of Liberton Brae. It set off slowly down the steepening grade, with the hapless crew vainly chasing behind. At the first bend it left the rails and ended up in the front garden of No. 40. There were only four passengers on the car – all elderly – but none was badly injured. One seventy year old, unscathed and unfazed, just continued her journey on the next tram!

This photograph was taken on Princes Street, with Maule's department store at the West End just in shot on the left. The architectural contrast is interesting, with the glaring whiteness of the British Linen Bank building, just a few years old, clashing with the plain frontages of the Georgian New Town houses. The first tram is on service No. 11, Braids to Stanley Road, while that following is on route 18, Newington station to Waverley via Melville Drive. The latter was one of the first routes to be axed after the Second World War – in March 1950 – as it was the worst revenue-earning service.

Edinburgh's trams crossed the Water of Leith no fewer than seven times within the city boundary. This concrete bridge, on Gorgie Road between Stenhouse Drive and Chesser Avenue, was the furthest upstream, and probably the newest (constructed 1927–9). The tramway extension from Gorgie to Stenhouse was opened on 20 July 1930, with this photograph taken very soon afterwards. Heading into town, the car is on service 3 to Newington station. Vegetation now almost obscures the bridge, with the brown brick block of Stevenson House obscuring the view of the distant Pentland Hills.

Staff outings were not always by charabanc. This group of employees is about to set off – probably in 1935 – from Leith's West Pier aboard the Hull-based Redcliffe Shipping Company's *Highland Queen*, formerly the *Brocklesby*. Astern is the renowned *Fair Maid*, which although launched in 1886 managed to survive until 1945! In the distance the unmistakable silhouette of the Victoria swing bridge can be discerned. Able to accommodate over 700 passengers, *Highland Queen* normally returned to her home port on the Humber in winter, doing so until 1936, her final season.

As mentioned in the introduction, the Tramway Department supported assorted social clubs, and for charitable events these organised fund-raising activities. Before the days of the National Health Service, flag days were held for both Edinburgh Royal Infirmary and Leith Hospital. For both events the department would provide decorated vehicles plus helpers. This is the effort of Tollcross tram depot's sports club for the 1934 Leith Hospital pageant. The red sandstone depot can be seen to the right.

The conductors' paying-in room at Tollcross depot. Woe betide any man with shortages (or overs!).

St Andrew Square from South St Andrew Street is, in this photograph, an oasis of calm order, with Lord Melville completing the symmetry atop his 135-foot high column. For some years this was the starting point for city tours. The 20-seat Morris coaches, new in 1930, were given an eye-catching bright red livery, the maroon element being confined to a strip below the windows.

One of the most popular city tours followed the Queen's Drive through Holyrood Park (or as it was then known, King's Park). A stop was made overlooking Duddingston Loch and village, seen here to good effect. This panorama shows the concentration of breweries around Craigmillar, and the open fields beyond which were soon to sprout a crop of dwellings to house families from the slum clearance areas in Dumbiedykes and St Leonard's.

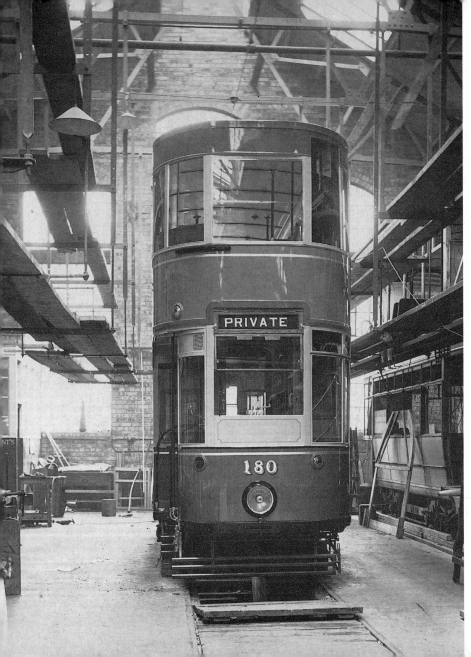

In April 1932 car 180 was the pride of the body shop and the last word in Edinburgh trams. It cost £4,000, which at today's values equates to approximately £140,000 (a new bus costs about £160,000, but generally has a life less than half that of a tram). The design was mostly that of Harry Mittell of the body department and incorporated many innovations – most of which were not repeated – meaning that this car remained unique. It was also remarkable for its livery, strikingly different from the normal maroon (madder) and white. The new car was painted bright red and grey, similar to the livery used on the Corporation's tour coaches, but never before or after used on a tram.

No. 180 was put under the charge of one of the most senior drivers, Fred B. Corsie, seen here on its platform. He retired in December 1934 after 42 years service. The following year 180 was repainted, losing its bright red distinctive style, which earned it the nickname 'Red Biddy'. Was it a coincidence that as soon as Corsie retired it was changed? Had the red livery been designed to link the perceived luxury of the coach fleet with that of the new tram?

Despite the positive impression created by Red Biddy, construction of the older style of car continued – perhaps to use up stocks of materials already bought in – but over the next two years several differing styles of tram were purchased from external suppliers. Twelve all-metal cars were ordered from three different suppliers. This is 241, one of six similar models by Metro–Cammell of Birmingham. As can be seen they were delivered in two halves, and remarkably not one pane of glass has been broken.

Twenty trams in this style were acquired next, again from three suppliers, all demonstrating this 'streamlined' appearance. No. 12 was from Messrs Hurst Nelson of Motherwell and is pictured when new at the top of Liberton Brae – the spot from where car 349 (page 30) had commenced its runaway adventure. On the horizon, left, can be seen the silhouette of Salisbury Crags, one of Edinburgh's most distinctive landmarks.

Eventually the Shrubhill designers produced this style of car, of which No. 69 was the first, appearing in 1934. The design then became standard and was built with few variations until 1950, the decision to abandon the trams following a year later. This picture was taken at the top of Craighall Road in Newhaven, which had no service from the end of the Leith Corporation independent era until October 1949, and was thus unused when the photograph was taken. The livery shown here was not perpetuated.

EOC seldom photographed vehicles other than those owned by the Corporation – or if he did neither negatives nor prints have survived. This is a Scottish Motor Traction Co. Leyland Titan on Waverley Bridge. Other transport subjects which he recorded included the narrow gauge Campbeltown to Machrihanish Railway, the Jersey Railway, and (one) shot of a London bus!

Daimler CF6 single deck bus No. 33 ascending the Mound with the castle and Princes Street forming the backdrop.

Construction intrigued EOC, as illustrated in this photograph of the rebuilding of the carriageway of the North Bridge with reinforced concrete. Steel-fixers are seen at work, and interestingly the deck is carried over beneath the footpath. Note the unusual base to the lamp standard. Normally this would have been formed by an extension of the pole, concreted into the ground, but this solution was not practical on the bridge.

In 1936 the Transport Department made a cine film featuring the diverse nature of its operations and social activities. Motorbus overhaul is being filmed here, with cameraman W. L. Russell on the bus roof. In 1953 he became general manager of Dundee Corporation Transport, and oversaw the closure of that city's tramways. This building had, many years before, housed the bodybuilding department of Edinburgh's horse tramways.

A rare view taken inside the old Waverley Market building at the east end of Princes Street. This was extensively used for exhibitions (the Ideal Home Exhibition was an annual fixture) as well as a Christmas carnival, and on many occasions the Transport Department provided a stand at road safety shows and other relevant events. Here the transport stall is on the right, complete with posters detailing showing times of the department's new film and advertising *New Speed* magazine. The central tableau relates to the School Dental Service.

Decorated and illuminated trams were a feature of Edinburgh's tramways from Christmas 1933 onwards when car 74, fitted with 2,500 coloured lamps, toured all routes. The more ambitious scheme illustrated here was produced for the May 1937 Coronation of King George VI and Queen Elizabeth. A withdrawn car (No. 40) was stripped down and an eighteen foot golden crown created, again brilliantly lit, making a very striking impression. Creating such displays gave employees a break from more routine departmental matters. A bus was also decorated, and all service buses had a crown or shield fitted to the lower saloon bulkhead.

When withdrawn from public service, car 221 ran in decorated guise featuring several different themes. Initially the main colour was silver, but later it was turned out in a golden hue. This photograph was taken in St Andrew Square in 1939 for 'Safety First Week'. The wording on the side actually reads 'It's Your Life Save It', but the emulsion of the negative cannot adequately separate the colours used for the apparently missing two words.

Central Garage staff photographed with a rank of Daimler COG6 double deck buses. This view appeared in *Speed*, captioned 'Some of the staff who, while the city sleeps, play their part in keeping the wheels turning'. By the end of the 1930s the Corporation had settled almost exclusively for Daimler buses, both single and double deck, the former being used only on routes with low clearance railway bridges. Various other makes were still owned, however, and many old Leyland Lions were to be see throughout the city, painted brown, stripped of their seats, in use as 'bothies' for repair gangs.